WHO WOULD WIN?®

ALLIGATOR

T0004384

vs.

PYTHON

BY
JERRY PALLOTTA
ILLUSTRATED BY
ROB BOLSTER

Scholastic Inc.

The publisher would like to thank the following for their
kind permission to use their photographs in this book:

Page 5 full-page image: FLPA / Alamy; page 10 bottom image: Biosphoto / SuperStock;
page 14 center image: Werner Bollmann / Getty Images; page 15 center image: Charles
McDougal / Ardea; page 19 full-page image: Michael & Patricia Fogden / Minden Pictures;
page 24 center image: kool99 / Getty Images; page 25 center image: taolmor / istock.

The fight in this book really has been happening in the Florida Everglades between the
American alligator and the Burmese python, an invasive species. Read all about it!

To Luke Beaulieu, Jackson Pallotta, Quinn Cronin, and Elsie Girard.
— J.P.
Dedicated to Mr. Andrew Wyeth.
— R.B.

ISBN: 978-0-545-45192-5

Text copyright © 2014 by Jerry Pallotta.
Illustrations copyright © 2014 by Rob Bolster.
All rights reserved. Published by Scholastic Inc.
SCHOLASTIC and associated logos are trademarks and/or registered trademarks of
Scholastic Inc. WHO WOULD WIN? is a registered trademark of Jerry Pallotta.

40 39   23 24

Printed in the U.S.A.   40
First printing, September 2014

What would happen if an alligator had a fight with a python? Wow—these are two deadly reptiles! Who is the toughest? Who do you think would win?

MEET THE ALLIGATOR

This is an American alligator. It can weigh up to 1,000 pounds. Scientific name: *Alligator mississippiensis.* These creatures live from Texas to North Carolina.

FACT
Alligators are reptiles.

DEFINITION
Reptiles are cold-blooded animals that have dry scales. Snakes, crocodiles, lizards, and turtles are also reptiles.

BIG FACT
The American alligator is the largest reptile in North America.

MEET THE PYTHON

This is a Burmese python. Scientific name: *Python bivittatus*. The Burmese python can grow up to 19 feet long. People have seen them swallow a deer, a cat, and a pig. Yikes!

FACT
Pythons are snakes.
Snakes are reptiles.

FANG FACT
Pythons are not venomous.
They have no poison.

ANCIENT FACT
Dinosaurs were also reptiles.

CROCODYLIA

There are four types of reptiles in an animal group called crocodylia.

CROCODILE

NOSE SHAPE TOP VIEW

Crocodiles have a V-shaped head. When they close their mouths, you can see a long bottom tooth.

ALLIGATOR

NOSE SHAPE TOP VIEW

Notice the wide head. When they close their wide mouths, you can't see the bottom teeth.

GAVIAL

NOSE SHAPE TOP VIEW

Gavials have a narrow, pointy snout. Great for catching fish!

CAIMAN

NOSE SHAPE TOP VIEW

The smallest crocodylian. A Cuvier's dwarf caiman is the smallest. All four types of crocodylia have lots of teeth!

We will use an American alligator to fight the Burmese python.

BIG SNAKES

The Burmese python is one of the five largest snakes in the world. Here are the other four:

RETICULATED PYTHON

The longest snake in the world. Yikes!

> ### LENGTH FACT
> *A reticulated python can be 30 feet long!*

GREEN ANACONDA

The heaviest snake in the world. Wow!

> ### WEIGHT FACT
> *A green anaconda can weigh almost 600 pounds!*

AFRICAN ROCK PYTHON

The biggest snake in Africa. Holy cow!

> ### DID YOU KNOW?
> *It can grow 20 feet long and weigh almost 200 pounds!*

SCRUB PYTHON

Another huge snake! Cool.

> ### COLORFUL FACT
> *Snakes come in every color.*

> ### SNAKE NUMBERS
> *There are about 3,000 known types of snakes in the world. Snakes have no arms and no legs. They have no moveable eyelids.*

BEHAVE!

The American alligator lives in North Carolina, South Carolina, Georgia, Florida, Alabama, Mississippi, Louisiana, and Texas. Most of these are warm Gulf Coast states.

> **ICE FACT**
> *An alligator would freeze to death in Alaska.*

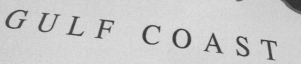

GULF COAST

where alligators live

Alligators love water. They live in ponds, lakes, rivers, estuaries, swamps, marshlands, and bayous. They tolerate a little salt water, and brackish water, but they prefer freshwater.

WE KNOW WHERE YOU LIVE!

The Burmese python lives in Southeast Asia. It got its name from Burma, which is now called Myanmar.

CHINA

BANGLADESH

INDIA

MYANMAR

LAOS

THAILAND

CAMBODIA

VIETNAM

where Burmese pythons live

MALAYSIA

BORNEO

INDONESIA

Oops! Some careless people let their pet Burmese pythons go in the Florida Everglades. Now the Everglades are overrun by pythons that don't belong here. They are an invasive species.

FLORIDA

THE EVERGLADES
A huge swampland full of water and tall grass in southern Florida.

DEFINITION
An invasive species is a plant or animal that lives somewhere that is not their natural habitat. Invasive species usually cause damage and upset the balance of nature.

SORRY!

Sorry, saltwater crocodile, you are the biggest, heaviest, scariest, and meanest of all crocodiles. But you are too big for this book. Saltwater crocodiles live in Australia. We'll save you for another *Who Would Win?* book. How about: *Saltwater Crocodile vs. Mosquito?*

SIZE FACT
Saltwater crocodiles can grow up to 20 feet long!

Here is an albino alligator.

DEFINITION
Albino means a lack of skin color.

YOU'RE OUT, TOO!

Here is the smallest snake in the world, the Barbados thread snake. It can't be in this book, either. Sorry, it's too small to fight the alligator.

actual size

REPTILE FACT
Some lizards—such as the island glass lizard—have no arms or legs. They may look like snakes, but they are legless lizards.

FACT
A flowerpot snake is also small.

Typical Burmese pythons have a color design similar to a giraffe. An albino Burmese python is mostly white but also has some color—usually light yellow and light orange.

TEETH

Alligators have a huge, strong jaw full of big teeth.
They have about 80 teeth, which are powerful weapons.

FACT
An alligator's jaw has the bite strength equal to 2,000 pounds per square inch. No human can lift 2,000 pounds. That's a ton!

TEETH TYPE
A dentist would say that alligators have conical-shaped teeth. Their teeth are shaped like an ice cream cone.

FANGS AND TEETH

Snakes don't chew their food. They have teeth designed to hold dinner. Slowly their strong, flexible jaws wiggle the food into their mouths, and they swallow it whole.

GOOFY QUESTION
Would you like to replace your teeth with a mouthful of fangs?

FANG TYPE
Snake fangs are shaped like curved knives.

Yikes! Burmese python teeth are sharp fangs that face inward. It is hard for an animal to escape the bite of a Burmese python.

ROLL— A GREAT TACTIC!

When an alligator gets hold of an animal, it rolls. This twists the animal and often breaks its arms or legs. An alligator is so strong, it can roll and rip its prey's limb off.

The roll is an amazing move. How do alligators learn it? We can only wonder.

NOT A FUN FACT
Yes, alligators have eaten a few people.

MIDNIGHT SNACK?
Alligators don't always eat the whole animal they catch. They often bury it and eat the rest later.

ENCIRCLE AND SQUEEZE, A DEADLY TECHNIQUE

Burmese pythons kill their prey by encircling them and squeezing them. They squeeze until the animal can't breathe.

OH NO!
Yes, Burmese pythons have eaten a few people.

DEFINITION
Snakes that squeeze their prey are called constrictors.

WARNING
Don't ever let someone put a python around your neck or on your shoulders.

ALLIGATOR TAIL

The alligator has a long, thick tail. The tail is almost as long as the rest of its body. It uses the tail to steer and swim.

SPEED LIMIT 30

WHACK!

SPEED FACT
Alligators can only run 30 miles per hour for a short distance.

DID YOU KNOW?
The alligator can also smack you with its tail.

Alligators are excellent swimmers. They can swim at 10 miles per hour.

DO SNAKES HAVE TAILS?

Not really. Its whole body is just shaped like a tail.
Pythons are also excellent swimmers.

Burmese pythons are faster in the water.
They can swim at 5 miles per hour.

FACT
*Burmese pythons have
about 4,000 muscles.*

HIDDEN

Can you find the alligator? He is well disguised in this swamp. The alligator patiently waits with his nose and eyes above water.

> ### FACT
> *Alligators cannot breathe underwater.*

> ### DID YOU KNOW?
> *Underwater, alligators close their nose and ears.*

> ### BONUS FACT
> *Usually an alligator holds its breath underwater for about 15 minutes.*

Alligators have been known to hold their breath for up to an hour. In cold water, an alligator can hold its breath even longer.

> ### QUESTION
> *Can alligators climb trees?*

CAMOUFLAGED

The Burmese python is also well disguised. It looks like leaves on the ground.

DID YOU KNOW?
The python also holds its eyes and nose above water.

LUNG FACT
A Burmese python can hold its breath underwater for at least a half hour.

Beware! Burmese pythons can climb trees.

THANK GOODNESS!
Alligators can't climb trees.

FOOD

Alligators eat insects, snails, fish, turtles, and other reptiles when they are young. As an alligator gets older, they eat larger creatures. A young alligator might get eaten by a big fish, hawk, or eagle. Hatchlings, watch out!

DEFINITION
A baby alligator is called a hatchling. Hatchlings eat insects and shrimp.

OLD
A grown-up alligator often goes out of the water to grab a huge mammal like a dog, a cow, or a horse.

FACT
Alligators are good at sneaking up on birds. They have been known to eat a duck, a goose, or an egret.

LET'S EAT

A Burmese python eats anything it can swallow whole.
A python can unhinge its jaw, stretch its ligaments, and
swallow something bigger than its mouth, usually small
mammals, frogs, and birds.

FACT

*A python
can taste,
smell, and
tell the
temperature
with its
tongue.*

PEOPLE EAT ALLIGATORS!

Some people eat alligators. You might find these menu items in some US Gulf Coast states:

Today's Specials

GRILLED ALLIGATOR STEAK

Juicy charcoal-broiled alligator steak, lightly seasoned, served with grits and fresh beet greens.

ALLIGATOR FINGERS AND FRENCH FRIES

Lightly breaded, deep-fried alligator strips, cooked until golden brown, served with crispy french fries.

BBQ ALLIGATOR

Slow-smoked gator fillets, dressed with our famous barbecue sauce, with creamy mashed potatoes, and choice of vegetable or crisp garden salad.

ALLIGATOR SAUSAGES

Hand-stuffed, ground alligator, seasoned with hot spices, served over rice, with roasted red pepper, sweet onion, and dijon mustard.

PEOPLE EAT PYTHONS, TOO!

Americans do not usually eat pythons. But some of us eat other snakes, such as rattlesnake. In other parts of the world people eat pythons. They say it is delicious.

ALLIGATOR SKIN

Many products are made from alligator skin. They include cowboy boots, belts, shoes, pants, and car seat covers.

ROUGH FACT
People say that an alligator's back skin feels like a bumpy truck tire.

Mirror, mirror, on the wall, who is the coolest reptile of all?

BELLY FACT
The alligator's belly skin is smooth.

DID YOU KNOW?
There is a fish called an alligator gar.

BURMESE PYTHON SKIN

Snakes have smooth, rugged skin. You can often identify a snake by the color and design of its skin.

FACT
Snakes are not slimy. They have dry, scaly skin.

Everglades alligator, you're not persuasive. I'll soon be king because I'm invasive.

DID YOU KNOW?
Snakes molt. As they grow larger, they shed their clear outer skin, usually in one piece.

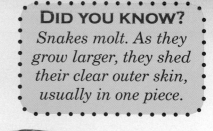

I SEE YOU

Alligators have excellent eyesight.

FEET

Alligators have strong legs, tough ugly feet, and long nails. They are great at digging holes to bury uneaten food, or dig pools of water.

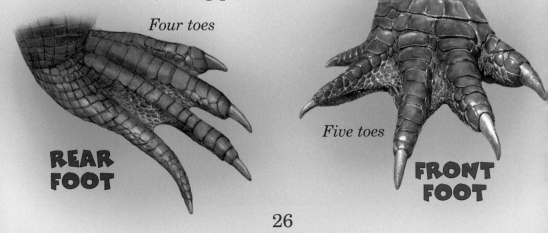

Four toes

Five toes

REAR FOOT

FRONT FOOT

I SENSE YOU

Python brains see a visual world and a thermal world.

DID YOU KNOW?
Pythons have heat sensors in their mouths. They can "see" your heat.

DEFINITION
Thermal means heat.

NO FEET

Snakes don't have feet. Snakes slither along the ground on their wide belly scales.

python belly scales
BOTTOM VIEW

A Burmese python and an alligator meet each other in the Florida Everglades.

The alligator bites the python. But the huge snake is not the type of food the alligator likes to eat. It has a strange feel. There are no limbs to rip off. He lets the snake go.

The python spins around and encircles the alligator.

The fight takes a long time. The snake starts squeezing the alligator. The alligator flips and tries to roll away.

The alligator tries to bite. The python slips away. After a long battle back and forth, the alligator gets tired.

The snake circles the alligator, then unhinges its jaw and starts swallowing the alligator. The python's strong jaw and throat muscles keep on pulling in the alligator.

The alligator can't breathe. The snake swallows the head. Then it swallows the alligator's body. Its legs are rugged and tough to eat.

The python finally gets the alligator's tail in its mouth. It's an ugly sight. The alligator is dead. The python has a bellyache. It will take a month for the python to digest it. But the python won this fight.

WHO HAS THE ADVANTAGE?
CHECKLIST

ALLIGATOR   **BURMESE PYTHON**

☐   Size   ☐

☐   Teeth or Fangs   ☐

☐   Camouflage   ☐

☐   Eyesight   ☐

☐   Tactics   ☐

☐   Speed   ☐

☐   Skin   ☐

Author note: This is one way the fight might have ended.
How would you write the ending?